CU00809886

April
Poems

Lawrence Wilson

To Blaise —

All best wishes
from your old
(very old) teacher —

Laurence
Wilson

Coeur Vert Press
2016

The April Poems

© 2016 by Lawrence Wilson
Coeur Vert Press
Mayfield, East Sussex
United Kingdom

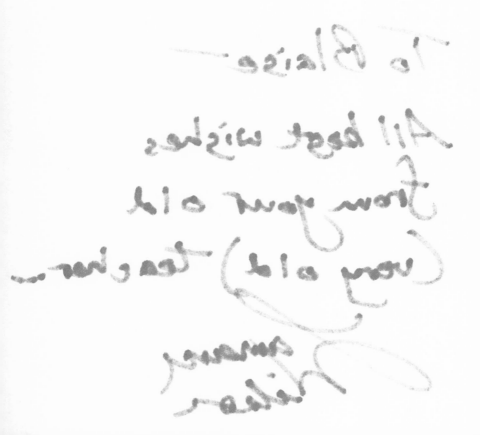

Lawrence Wilson

Introduction

I find a certain artistic satisfaction in exploring traditional formal forms of poetry while incorporating vernacular language. I write a lot of sonnets (like days 1, 2, 5, 9, 10, etc) in a 6/6/2 form that I've dubbed "Hackerian" after the poet Marilyn Hacker, who devised several alternatives to the Shakespearian standard. Not as difficult as might be imagined. A goodly portion of spoken English is iambic. Our hearts beat in iambs…

You'll also find a sprinkling of other formal forms—a villanelle, a triolet, a sestina, a series of linked haiku, some variations on the cinquain—as well as some blank verse and a couple of pantoums (days 6 and 15), which is a Malaysian form where lines repeat in a strict mathematical pattern. A favourite mode of mine, one with which few are familiar, I call the aiken (days 7, 11, 16, 21, 23 and 29), after Rye-born writer Joan Aiken, who used it for a character's poems in her novel *Foul Matter*. It appears to be based, at least partially, on an ancient Greek dramatic form, and I like the unequal lengths of line combined with the unexpected syncopated rhyme scheme.

And, by popular demand, there's even a limerick. I tried, at first, to make it a tragic one, just to see if it could be done—but it twisted in my hand and went amusing instead. As they do.

This collection would not have come about without the encouragement of Sarah Miles of Paper Swans Press. In late March 2016, Sarah challenged her growing cadre of poets to write a poem every day for the thirty days of April as a way of celebrating National Poetry Month. I don't know who else took her up on it, but my sincere thanks to a brilliant writer, editor and generator of ideas.

But even greater thanks go to my partner-in-life Paul Camic, without whose loving support none of this would have been possible. I thank him for the time to write and for things to write about.

1

Concrete Thinking
(for G Moore)

"I hate this stuff," she said, "these similes
and metaphors—the girl is just a girl!
She's not a wild rose! Why does the poet
call her that? A girl's a girl, a plant's
a plant. It makes no sense. Comparisons
like that? Misleading! Simply say what's so!"

"The poet is trying to," I told her. "See
how imagery contributes? It is your
decision: see or not, but there is more
to word-craft than reality. You can't
dismiss the art. When all is said and done
you like it or you don't—but this I know

the poet's shared his vision." "Big fat deal!
Pretentious nonsense—show me something real!"

In Response to Your Sleepy Questions

it's half past five, the sun an hour away
from rising, eastern sky the colour of
an unripe peach, a chilly wind demanding
scarf around my neck. The streetlamps dark
the pavements empty—only up because
the agèd dog requires a comfort break

but now the peach is ripening—it may
turn out to be a morning warm and lovely
if those streaks of pink and lemon can
indeed be trusted. Saturday...no work
no chores, no schedule. I must sleep just
a little more, but not make the mistake

of missing skies of endless silver-blue
by lingering too long in bed with you

3

A Triolet for Good Friends

another simple, extraordinary Sunday
sleeping late, a nice pub lunch, wine
(blue skies thickening late to stormy grey)
another simple, extraordinary Sunday
work, routine, a thousand years away
(and if it rains all night, I don't mind)
another simple, extraordinary Sunday
sleeping late, a nice pub lunch, wine

Monday Morning Villanelle

Monday morning in a pretty coastal town
high, thin, tissue-paper clouds, streaks of blue sky
the early train is in—tourists hurrying down

with rolling cases, plastic bags of souvenirs found
in antique shops, gift boutiques—so much to buy
on weekend mornings in a pretty coastal town

cafés just opening, black rubbish bags round
and bulging, seagulls fleeing as families stampede by
the early train is in—tourists hurrying down

and business-men and -women, London-bound
they'll be there in an hour! The trains practically fly
on Monday morning, fleeing this pretty coastal town

but I am lucky—not going anywhere! We've found
a perfect *pied-à-terre*, tiny, affordable to buy
the early train is in—tourists hurrying down

so desperate not to miss it. The whistle sounds
their holiday is over, poor things, but I
may enjoy my Monday morning in this pretty coastal town
while the early train pulls away, taking the tourists down

Conversational Sonnet

"My eye is caught on fragile things today,"
he said. "I don't know why—I am not ill,
or melancholic, but—it's just that—look,
those tiny scarlet leaves unfolding, and
that wren, so vulnerable, yet fearless! She—
Oh, why do words elude me? Tongue in knots

I can't say what I really need to say."
"Don't castigate yourself," I told him. "Will
the wren thrive just because you've found a bookish
metaphor? Let go. Breathe deep. The land
awakens to another spring, and we
can never know how many more we've got."

"Now, that's morose," he sighed. "A sombre mood."
"Then re-define it—call it gratitude."

another cup of tea, another rhymed description
another glance through window-glass
new leaves, wind-danced, sun-gilded
all warm yellow amber, all silver-silk blue

another glance through window-glass
rain is coming, but for now
all warm yellow amber, all silver-silk blue
a benison, a blessing, an invitation

rain is coming, but for now
the birds are singing, and hyacinths scent the garden
a benison, a blessing, an invitation
flee pen and paper—run, shout, sing aloud

the birds are singing, and hyacinths scent the garden
another cup of tea, another rhymed description
flee pen and paper—run, shout, sing aloud
new leaves, wind-danced, sun-gilded

Perseverance

each day I pass the rich, dark square of soil
where, weeks ago, I scattered seeds on trust
some fine as dust

and rain has fallen, sun has warmed it daily
but still no evidence of fragile green
is to be seen

I'm not a novice gardener, just impatient
the winter was too long, the skies too grey
and so today

I'm hungry, hunting for the new beginnings:
anemones and bluebells, beech leaves green
as tourmaline

and, in my garden, proof of spring's renaissance
the yearly miracle, the silent shout
of sprig and sprout

8

today: the eastern sky afire with gold
the marshes green, a thousand baaing sheep
our friend Odile arrives by early train
from Paris, and we spend the day in chat
and walks and buying chocolate, souvenirs
and wine, then dinner at the Landgate Bistro—
not a cloud, nor raindrop in the sky
just chilly stars to guide us home to bed

A Sonnet for Hastings

in Old Town Hastings, rainy Saturday
so in and out: museum, junk shops, stores
exploring stony beach and patient boats
the seagulls picking over gutted fish
and up the High Street, down the other side
pink wine, and cheese, a cake knife, scented soap

and still the rain clouds lingered, purling grey
a restaurant that we'd liked had closed its doors
so lunch was Cornish pasties. Soaking coats
and bags, but—honestly?—I wouldn't wish
for sun, not if it meant we might decide
to give the town a miss. I live in hope

that every time we visit there, we find
as much to bring delight to heart and mind

10

£2.49 Per Packet

"viola odorata"—violet seeds
to sprinkle in-between, in cracks, behind
the more important plants, and (fingers crossed)
they'll rush to germinate and grow and bloom
I cannot think it spring without their scent
and if they hide successfully, ignored

by those who (wrongly) think them nasty weeds
they'll multiply, and very soon I'll find
them everywhere—a legion!—at a cost
of two pounds forty-nine. Just give them room
and soil and rain, a kiss of sun, and plenty
more will smile next spring: a perfumed horde

of modest vandals, hardy, hidden spies
who'll hide from unappreciative eyes

Still Life with Very Old Dog

behind the wicker chair, a private corner
discarded towels in disordered heaps
the old dog sleeps

we used to find her curled on the sofa
this last twelvemonth she can no longer leap
and so she'll sleep

on Oriental rugs or hallway carpet
a lambkin girl, all whites and curly creams
the old dog dreams

and semi-barks, and twitches, chasing squirrels
or burglars—she has promises to keep
our girl, asleep

to love us and protect us. In her dotage
she's not forgotten obligations deep
good dog! Asleep

the day will come when she will not awaken
for now we care for her as best we can
she needs a hand

in rising, walking—medicines in cheddar
can't climb a stair or even kerb too steep
old girl, asleep

who trusts us, as she has for sixteen summers
and when, at last, it's time for her to go
I trust we'll know

Soliloquy
(To the Lady in the Powder-Blue Nissan Micra Just Ahead of Me)

Perhaps you hadn't realised, but you've
Been driving thirty in a sixty mile
Per hour zone for twenty minutes. Hate
To be the bearer of bad news, but it
Is possible to do a decent speed
Uphill, 'round curves and bends, and even when
A vehicle approaches in the other
Lane. Now, several explanations come
To mind that could excuse the way you drive:
Timidity, or inexperience
Or sheer oblivion—I think the third
Most likely, as you've never glanced in rear-
View mirror to observe the massive queue
Of vehicles behind you, drivers forced
To crawl along at speeds grandmotherly.
A busy road—unsafe to pass you but
You could pull over, let us all get by.
You could, if you were not a timid fool,
Or blind, or impolite—all three? You could
Speed up. You could turn off—is that a Tesco
Up ahead? You could just crash your car
And die. Such fine solutions to the problem!
None of us will mind which one you choose.
But I can almost hear your crabby voice:
"Oh, sixty is the LIMIT! I am free
To drive at any speed I please, as long
As I do not exceed the LIMIT!" True,
As we, the thirty drivers stuck behind,
Are free to curse you—not that you will hear...
You could pull over, could speed up. You won't.
Another mile at thirty miles per hour,
Another, and another... Damn you, ma'am!
The road is straight, the surface dry. You could
Speed up. You could speed up. You could. You won't.

13

at four AM, the fog pours through the streets
like dirty water from a jug, as cold
as thick, as clinging. Four AM: the gulls
are silent, daily screaming still to come
delivery van, its headlamps glowing gold
a monster in the mist, disgorging bread

and eggs to restaurants. I never meet
a soul at four—just me, the dog, the old
night thinning towards a distant dawn, the dulled
sky blackish-grey. I never hear the hum
of streetlamps any other time. The cold
insistent—dog is finished—back to bed

to wake at eight. The fog has fled. The sky
a turquoise bowl inverted, thin clouds high

it's April, and the Wealden gods have turned
the gas to "high" and struck a match. The flames
of lapis flicker—catch—and spread until
the forest floor is blue, a burning stove
of flowers, and we walk through scented clouds
as if our feet were tangled up in sky

a week or two the bluebell woods will burn
with colour, then, too quickly, time to tame
the hyacinth inferno. Trees will fill
with fragile green, full shade engulf the groves
so take the time today—a morning loud
with birdsong, bright with sun. Delight your eyes

and ears and nose, enjoy the yearly view
this temporary miracle of blue

15

Muscle Memory

wet clay spinning between my fingers
first time in eleven years
the body remembers
the push, the pull, the satisfaction of centering

first time in eleven years
the joy of mud!
the push, the pull, the satisfaction of centering
and a cylinder rises as high as my elbow

the joy of mud
wet clay spinning between my fingers
and a cylinder rises as high as my elbow
the body remembers

At the Wine Bar

we came for "just a glass before the movie"
and stayed for conversation festive, bright
an appetite

for jokes and chat, for dinner plans and grumbles
for dreams and wishes, gentle melodies
and mockeries

a glass of liquid red or white or rosé
a slap on back, a welcoming embrace
a friendly place

"How is your dog?" "Come out for Chinese dumplings!"
"That man in Watchbell Street..." "My recipe
for kedgeree"

when we walked in, the room was packed with people
the clock has struck eleven, crowd has thinned
goodbyes begin

a half an inch of wine in all our glasses
another round? Or shall we just go home?
in pairs? Alone?

Plus and Minus

a blaze
of molten sun
the bedroom floods with light
a large obnoxious tenor singing
"Nessun dorma!" and reluctantly
we wake and stumble—"Coffee? Tea?"
to kitchen, grumbling
a shower, toast
a sigh

a walk
the temperature
is cool despite the sun
the Sunday papers under arm
the dog in major sniffing-mode, and slow
"A plaice for lunch today, perhaps?"
while gazing at the view
of river, sky
and you

I passed that rock on Saxonbury Hill
today, the one that's cleft, a half-height door
I always wonder what's beyond—what hall
what mountain-king... It's hard to see behind
its screen of branches—one must know the place
and watch for shadow, not turn head away

I'd like to stop the car, explore...until
that day, I'll fantasise: the goblin wars
the opal mines, the crystal waterfalls...
an ancient ring-fort crowns the hill—I'll find
the treasure in its caverns, win the race
to free the captive wizard, save the day...

or not. No doubt it's just a curious stone
unlikely to be hiding dragon bone

Linked Haiku

fat slice of cheddar
gibbous moon in midnight sky
straining towards the full

straining towards the full
unwilling to stay crescent
lopsided white smile

lopsided white smile
who is that star you dance with
across black marble?

across black marble
somersault to horizon
joker moon, grinning

joker moon, grinning
offer me silence, sweet dreams
sustenance in sleep

sustenance in sleep
sink towards western distant hills
flee the glowing east

flee the glowing east
but rise again tomorrow
fatter sliced cheddar

Staff, After

"tea?
sugar?
drop of milk?"
sweet amber silk!
soothing throat after long day in classroom

"cake?
sandwich?"
none for me
just my hot tea
weary, cheerful grumbles in the staffroom

"prep
tonight?"
sharp pen poised
don't dare make noise
teachers known to snap—no hesitation

"bye!"
"good night!"
school ends—rush
descends the hush
still corridors, patient isolation

ERII

I keep the lady's pictures in my pocket
in wallet, folded, pink and blue and green
long live the Queen

I've never met her, and it isn't likely
that she'll reward me with a knightly badge
God save Her Maj

there's subtle comfort in a jewelled tiara
in pearls and platinum, aquamarines
long live our Queen

a comfort in uninterrupted reigning
I can't define precisely why that it is
but God save Liz

fragility, endurance in one package
that quote: "I say to you that my whole life..."
(long live Phil's wife)

"...shall be devoted to your service..." Forthright
declared when she was only twenty-one
that's how it's done

the labour has been long, and I applaud her
it's hard to say exactly what I mean
God save the Queen

Conversation with a Cynic

"cholesterol is bad for you? That's just
a myth," he said. "The evidence is thin
the science flawed. Your body needs the fat
so don't ignore the hamburgers with cheese
I wouldn't say the same for salt or wine
but do enjoy some butter with your bread"

"so strange what people think," I told him. "Must
the science languish and illogic win?
those holy books? Just stories—earth's not flat
and Father Adam never met his Eve
no UFOs, no ghosts—vaccines are fine
and bottled water same as tap. Instead

of mere belief, could not we strive for thought?"
"We could," he smiled, "could it be sold and bought"

a dragon slain in far-off Cappadocia
a maiden saved with fine knightly restraint
the guy's a saint!

can't help but think we've heard this story elsewhere
Andromeda and Perseus? The tale
does not go stale

though part of me'd enjoy some gender-bending
the princess saves the prince from harm this time
a twist sublime

but one we rarely read in tales collected
no room for Saint Georgina on this isle
(though I would smile)

I run my fingertips along their spines
and each one tells a story, open, shut
each volume, upright, leaning, stacked in piles
each one familiar, murmuring its tale
in voices multiplied by thousands. Private
library of Lawrence Wilson, Esq!

I've read a few a double-dozen times
returned to worlds familiar with what
can only be described as joy, and while
I read, the mundane disappears (or fails
at least, to make impact). My dragons, pirates
runaways and lovers—evidence

in ink and paper of a life immersed
in sweet imagination, last to first

this April is more like November
and we're all in a dismal grey temper
with warmth incongruent
the sun's playing truant
it's colder than I can remember

my parka's pressed back into service
I'm shivering like a stalled dervish
it's practically May
and I'm sorry to say
that the temperature's going to get worse-ish

Learning

a kick-and-sell performer, that was me
a voice to fill a theatre to the gods
a bit of tap, ballet, a little jazz
the classics: Rodgers, Hammerstein, and Kern
and complicated stuff like Sondheim, Brecht
the joys of centre-stage, spot-lit, and loud

and then one day at university
the acting teacher cast me 'gainst the odds
a play by Shakespeare. Stupifaction. "Has
he lost his mind?" But I was swift to learn
that I could speak the verse with due respect
that I was good—an actor, not a clod

who entertained and thought it was enough
"what fools these mortals be!" Yeah, that's the stuff

Sway

so—every Wednesday, storytelling time
the littlest ones, of seven, eight, arrange
themselves on comfy cushions 'round my feet
and I start spinning age-old tales, from Grimm
and Andersen, Perrault—today the myth
of Demeter and lost Persephone

they didn't know the story, which was fine
much better when they don't. The tale's strange
enough without the interruptions. Sweet-
faced, round-eyed, listening to the myth, a hymn
to otherness, to bad behaviour with
a godly twist. The story's ended—see

them all, unbidden, start to stamp and sing
to wake the goddess and bring back the spring

28

Cuppa

sometimes I think the second cup of tea
each morning is the best—the first to wake
me up, the second to enjoy; the first
is function, second luxury. An hour
from rising, I must dash for work, and once
I'm there and brewed a second cup, the thrill

is gone. Another brewed late morning, free
for half an hour. Biscuit. Apple. Take
one back to desk. It's not exactly thirst
which drives me, more the caffeinated power
so brown, a milky-sweet beneficence
a swift rejuvenation. Habit. Fill

the cup. Refill it if I have the time
and burn my tongue on beverage sublime

there was a time when I could not imagine
a day without you in it—such good friends!
but these things end

our paths diverged. Our interests led us elsewhere
I saw you last in 1989
a younger time

before the Internet, before an email
could bounce across the sea and "ping" your phone
if we'd have known

that we would never meet again in person
would we have parted differently? I'd like
to think we might

you're famous now in western Massachusetts
they know me in this little Sussex town
and I have found

as you have, pleasant friendships beyond measure
and love to warm the heart for all our lives
my man, your wife

and twenty-seven years without a letter
without a card at Christmas. Birthdays? Nil
but somehow, still

the bonds we wove when we were young and callow
connect us even now, a gentler flame
that warms your name

a friend is still a friend, though distance widens
in time and space. My brother-of-the-heart
wide world apart

30

May Eve

another ordinary Saturday
the weekly shopping done, the laundry folded
some sun, some cloud-shadow—it may rain tonight
no invitations, nothing in the post of interest
a pot of tea, perhaps a walk to the bluebell woods
and another chapter of that novel read

but in my heart's mind and memory, a risky day, red-
lettered on the calendar, a day
perhaps, to walk warily in the woods
a night, perhaps, when strange dreams might unfold
so slip sideways, catch no one's eye or interest—
we're halfway 'round from Hallowe'en, and the fairies ride tonight

a laughing host in silvered silks, wrapped in night's
dimmed colours under a waning moon. A dream…perhaps I read
about it when I was a child—always been interested
in such folklore—or perhaps it was a tale told at end of day
by a loving granny—kiss on forehead, enfolding
hug to keep me safe when walking in the dream-woods

"the apple is always your friend—the holly a chancy wood
avoid the elder-tree, especially at night"
whose tongue whispered this? Whose wisdom, folded
into child-sized bites? I've always read
fairy-stories, but all this curious advice—by day
faintly ridiculous, nothing to interest

a logical adult—yet I am interested
cautious—fearful, even, sometimes. Wonder-struck. I would
never assume that you think this a special day—
not the same books, not the same granny—so tonight
you'll probably leave no bowl of milk outside, no red
berries on your lintel, no eyes folded

sensibly shut while the cavalcade passes, enfolded
in mist and shadow… You're not really interested
are you? Not for you the iced golden wine, the rare red
meat of dream and battle. If I tell you that the woods
breathe danger from their roots tonight
you'll laugh—easy enough to do by day

but when the last day
        of April falters and folds
when eyes in the night
        open wide, and watch with hungry interest
then clutch your charm of rowan-wood
        and remember what you've read

I grew up near Chicago, Illinois, and have degrees in drama, education and interdisciplinary art. I moved to the UK in 2005, and currently teach English and drama at Rose Hill, one of the oldest independent prep schools in England.

I have sung and acted professionally and have exhibited my pottery, sculpture, installations and artist's books in the UK and the USA and online. My fiction, poetry, essays and reviews have appeared in *Albedo One, Agenda, The Darker Side of Love, Poet's Cove, Art and Academe, Prairie Light Review, The Art of Monhegan Island,* on Salon.com, Monhegan.com and in other journals and collections.

Cover image, "Mad Tulip," and author photo
by Lawrence Wilson

Printed in Baskerville,
a serif typeface designed by John Baskerville in 1757